■ SCHOLASTIC

SIGHT WORD SONG BOOK

Liza Charlesworth

New York • Toronto • London • Auckland • Sydney
Mexico City • New Delhi • Hong Kong • Buenos Aires

D1404677

For my three lads, Justin, Dash & Theo—
who taught me volumes about the magic of music.

–LC

Song Lyrics: Copyright © Liza Charlesworth

Arranged and produced by John Marshall Media.
Pages 15–39: Directed by Robin Lai. Engineered and mixed by Eric Dabdoub.
Female vocal: Cassandra Kubinski; Male vocal: Daniel Johnson
Pages 40–64: Directed and mixed by Eric Dabdoub.
Female vocal: Shayna Davies; Male vocal: Daniel J. Edwards

Design: Tannaz Fassihi
Illustration: Michael Robertson

ISBN: 978-1-338-31079-1
First printing, June 2019.

2 3 4 5 6 7 8 9 10   40   25 24 23 22 21 20 19

Table of Contents

TEACHING TIPS

SONGS

Introduction

The, of, you, been, into, and *would* are examples of sight words. Research shows that as much as 70 percent of everything we read is made up of sight words—those bland connective words that are essential to text, but usually a challenge to define and decode. Research also shows that children with the ability to automatically recognize sight words are on course to be agile, confident readers. But with a school day already jam-packed with curriculum, how do busy educators find time to focus on these essential words?

Welcome to the *Sight Word Song Book*! This entertaining teaching tool will help your students master the first 100 sight words from the Fry List in just minutes a day. Why is this simple resource so effective? Because it teaches the target sight words via the brain-gaining combination of (visual) texts and (auditory) songs. And since these "piggyback" songs are based on favorite tunes, your students will learn them in a snap. So what are you waiting for? Add these playful tunes to your classroom mix and watch your students sing their way to reading success!

Featured Sight Words

The songs in this book teach the top 100 sight words from the Fry List:

the	at	there	some	my
of	be	use	her	than
and	this	an	would	first
a	have	each	make	water
to	from	which	like	been
in	or	she	him	call
is	one	do	into	who
you	had	how	time	am
that	by	their	has	its
it	words	if	look	now
he	but	will	two	find
was	not	up	more	long
for	what	other	write	down
on	all	about	go	day
are	were	out	see	did
as	we	many	number	get
with	when	then	no	come
his	your	them	way	made
they	can	these	could	may
I	said	so	people	part

Sight Word Song Book © Liza Charlesworth, Scholastic Inc.

Teaching Routine

To get the most out of the *Sight Word Song Book*, follow these simple teaching tips.

BEFORE SINGING

1. Choose a song to share and review its customized lesson plan. (See pages 7–14.) The songs can be introduced in any order you choose.

2. Preview the song to familiarize yourself with the tune and lyrics. You can download audio of all the songs at **www.scholastic.com/sightwordsongbook** by entering your email address and this code: **SC831709**.

3. Share the appropriate lyric page with students. You can copy the lyrics onto chart paper, make a photocopy of the song from this book, or download a PDF at the link above. The PDF will enable you to share the song with the entire class via your projector and whiteboard.

WHILE SINGING

1. Call children's attention to the lyric page. Point out the title and illustration, encouraging them to predict what the song might be about. Discuss the meaning of any new vocabulary words, such as *carousel*, *gallop*, *coral*, or *slurp*.

2. Share the song's two featured sight words, which appear in the upper-right corner. Read them aloud and write them in the air together. Explain that the words will appear several times in the song.

3. Sing the song together. If you are sharing an enlarged lyric page, run your finger, or a pointer, under the text as you do.

4. Discuss the song. Build literacy skills by sharing one or all of the song's Comprehension Boosters. (See pages 7–14.)

5. Have a sight word hunt! Challenge students to circle the two featured sight words in the song. (TIP: Consider using two different-color crayons or pens to underline each sight word.)

6. Sing the song several times, encouraging children to listen and look for each underlined sight word as you do. To reinforce learning, invite children to clap each time one of the featured sight words is encountered.

Connection to the Standards

The activities in this book support the standards for Reading: Foundational Skills for students in grades K–2.

Foundational Skills
Read common high-frequency words by sight.

Print Concepts
Demonstrate understanding of the organization and basic features of print.

Phonological Awareness
Demonstrate understanding of spoken words, syllables, and sounds (phonemes).

Fluency
Read with sufficient accuracy and fluency to support comprehension.

Speaking and Listening
Participate in collaborative conversations about age-appropriate topics.

Source: Copyright 2010 National Governors Association Center for Best Practices and Council of Chief State School Officers. All rights reserved.

AFTER SINGING

1. "Innovate the text" by replacing some of the song's key words with new ones. For example, in "Monster Food," you can replace one or all of the monster foods mentioned with new ones, such as "slimy snails" or "banana peels." For added fun, encourage students to suggest ideas—the sillier the better! When you're done, sing your new version together.

2. Revisit the song at a later date. Each time you sing it, you'll help hardwire children's sight word recognition skills.

3. Place a binder filled with reproducible versions of the song lyrics—along with link to the audio—in your listening center for children to enjoy on their own or with partners.

10 Great Ways to Share Sight Word Songs

1. Start each day with a song! Share a tune during circle time or morning meeting to wake up kids' brain cells for a great day of learning.

2. Invite partners to learn a song together and teach it to the rest of the class.

3. Transition from one activity to the next by re-singing a familiar song. This will energize children to dive into their next lesson with zest.

4. Encourage individual students or groups to record themselves singing the songs on an iPad or tape recorder. Place those recordings in your listening center, along with reproducible lyric pages, for other children to enjoy.

5. Teach your students several of the sight words songs, then perform them for other classes.

6. Challenge children to carefully copy the lyrics of one or more sight word songs onto lined paper. Not only will this help hardwire the sight words, it will improve kids' handwriting skills, too.

7. Make the singing experience kinesthetic by acting the songs out or embellishing them with simple hand gestures.

8. Have a sight word dance party. Play several songs and invite kids to dance, dance, dance!

9. Before the bell rings, share a song as an end-of-the-day treat.

10. Once children have learned a song, send home lyrics pages so they can sing the tunes along with their loved ones.

Song-by-Song Lesson Plans

To extend learning with each song, use these instant lesson plans.

Monster Food

Sight Words: *he, and*

Vocabulary Word: *gobble*

Comprehension Boosters:

1. What is the monster's name?

2. Do you think monster food is great? How is it different from people food?

Innovating the Text:
Copy the lyrics onto chart paper and replace the monster foods mentioned in the song with new ones, such as "slimy snails" or "banana peels." Then sing your new version together!

The Sneaky Snake

Sight Words: *there, was*

Vocabulary Words: *sneaky, bellyache*

Comprehension Boosters:

1. How was the snake sneaky?

2. Why did the snake get a bellyache?

Innovating the Text:
Copy the lyrics onto chart paper and replace the word "cake" with another baked treat, such as "pie." Then sing your new version together!

The Cookie Boy

Sight Words: *the, said*

Vocabulary Words: *clever, lickety-split*

Comprehension Boosters:

1. What folktale is the song about? (*The Gingerbread Boy*)

2. Was the cookie boy right when he said, "You'll never catch me"?

Innovating the Text:
Copy the lyrics onto chart paper and replace the lines "I'll eat you today" and "CRUNCH!" with new ones, such as "We'll go swimming today" and "SPLASH!" Then sing your new version together!

Gilly Ghosty

Sight Words: *is, when*

Vocabulary Words: *holler, babble*

Comprehension Boosters:

1. What made Gilly Ghosty sad?

2. What made Gilly Ghosty happy?

Innovating the Text:
Copy the lyrics onto chart paper and replace the phrases "gets a little hungry" and "gets a little bottle" with new ones, such as "gets a little sleepy" and "gets a little naptime" Then sing your new version together!

Pirate Song

Sight Words: *use, words*

Vocabulary Words: *mate, aye, scallywag, blimey, yo ho ho, thar she blows, arghh*

Comprehension Boosters:

1. Can you find all the pirate words in the poem? What do they mean?

2. Would you like to be a pirate? Why or why not?

Innovating the Text:
Copy the lyrics onto chart paper and replace some of the pirate words with new, real or imagined ones, such as "Ahoy" or "Blumber-smit!" Then sing your new version together!

Furry Little Mice

Sight Words: *we, are*

Vocabulary Words: *squeak, eek*

Comprehension Boosters:

1. Why do you think people scream "EEK" when they see mice?

2. Can you think of some good words to describe mice? Make a list.

Innovating the Text:
Copy the lyrics onto chart paper and replace the sentence "We are cute and we can squeak" with a new one, such as "We eat cheese and we are sweet." Then sing your new version together!

Ben's Band

Sight Words: *his, their*

Vocabulary Words:
banjo, crescent

Comprehension Boosters:
1. Do you remember all the animals in Ben's band? What are their names?
2. Does Ben's band sing this song during the day or at night? How do you know?

Innovating the Text:
Copy the lyrics onto chart paper and replace some or all of the band animals—plus their names—with new ones, such as "a horse whose name was Harry," or "a duck whose name was Dora." (Don't forget to change the animal sounds they make, too.) Then sing your new version together!

Where Is Humpty?

Sight Words: *what, as*

Vocabulary Words:
oops, tumbled

Comprehension Boosters:
1. Do you know the original Humpty Dumpty rhyme? Recite it together.
2. Humpty had an accident. What happened?

Innovating the Text:
Copy the lyrics onto chart paper and replace the word "tumbled" with another word for *fall*, such as "toppled." Then sing your new version together!

The Talking Gnu

Sight Words: *do, you*

Vocabulary Words: *gnu, chatty*

Comprehension Boosters:
1. Where does the gnu live? What is his name?
2. Is this song about a real or pretend gnu? How do you know?

Innovating the Text:
Copy the lyrics onto chart paper and replace the word "gnu" with another type of animal, such as "bear." Then sing your new version together!

On Top of My Sandwich

Sight Words: *I, on*

Vocabulary Words:
gumdrops, mustard

Comprehension Boosters:
1. Can you remember all the food items in this sandwich? Make a list.
2. Why do you think the sandwich-maker's big brother does NOT take a bite of the sandwich?

Innovating the Text:
Copy the lyrics onto chart paper and replace some or all of the sandwich ingredients with new ones, such as "pizza" or "cupcakes." Then sing your new version together!

Mary Had a Hairy Ape

Sight Words: *a, she*

Vocabulary Words: *ape, guitar*

Comprehension Boosters:
1. What nursery rhyme is this song like? (*Mary Had a Little Lamb*) Recite it together.
2. What happens when Mary gives the ape a guitar?

Innovating the Text:
Copy the lyrics onto chart paper and replace the word "ape" with another kind of animal, such as "sloth." Then sing your new version together!

Read Your Book

Sight Words: *your, this*

Vocabulary Words: *plant, slipper*

Comprehension Boosters:
1. What fairytale is described in each stanza? (1. *The Three Little Pigs*; 2. *The Frog Prince*; 3. *Jack and the Beanstalk*; 4. *Cinderella*)
2. What is your favorite fairytale? Tell about it.

Innovating the Text:
Copy the lyrics onto chart paper and replace a book description with a new one, such as "It's about a little hen who makes a loaf of bread." (*The Little Red Hen*) Then sing your new version together!

Pete Penguin

Sight Words: *by, with*

Vocabulary Words:
waddled, sea

Comprehension Boosters:
1. What activities does Pete Penguin invite his new friend to do with him?
2. Would you like to play with Pete Penguin? What would you do?

Innovating the Text:
Copy the lyrics onto chart paper and replace the phrase "We can skate and sled and ski" with a new one, such as "We can build a snowman." Then sing your new version together!

Ruby Robin

Sight Words: *can, be*

Vocabulary Words: *flutter, supper*

Comprehension Boosters:

1. What color is a ruby? Why is Ruby a great name for a robin?

2. Why doesn't the child want to stay for supper?

Innovating the Text: Copy the lyrics onto chart paper and replace the word "worm" with a new bird food, such as "beetle." Then sing your new version together!

Goldilocks, Goldilocks

Sight Word: *not, in*

Vocabulary Words: *porridge, snooze*

Comprehension Boosters:

1. What fairytale is this song about? (*Goldilocks and the Three Bears*)

2. Why does Goldilocks run away forever?

Innovating the Text: Copy the lyrics onto chart paper and replace the line "You'll eat porridge, break a chair, snooze in bed and wake to bears" with a new one, such as "You'll eat popcorn, break a toy, read a book, and wake to snakes." Then sing your new version together!

Little Dot

Sight Word: *all, were*

Vocabulary Words: *stomped, extinct*

Comprehension Boosters:

1. Why is Little Dot a funny name for a dinosaur?

2. Would you like to have a dinosaur join your class today? Why or why not?

Innovating the Text: Copy the lyrics onto chart paper and replace the line "Dot loved reading and math" with a new one, such as "Dot loved writing and art." Then sing your new version together!

Frog and Dog

Sight Word: *if, it*

Vocabulary Words: *ribbit, yappy*

Comprehension Boosters:

1. What do frogs say? What do dogs say?

2. How are frogs and dogs alike? How are they different?

Innovating the Text: Copy the lyrics onto chart paper and replace the word "frog" and his attributes (jump/swim/play/say "ribbit" with new ones in order to write an original verse about the animal of your choice. Then sing your new version together!

Orange Orangutan

Sight Word: *each, an*

Vocabulary Words: *orangutan, jungle, vines*

Comprehension Boosters:

1. What color is this orangutan? What vehicle does he drive?

2. Would you like to swing on vines with Tarzan? Why or why not?

Innovating the Text: Copy the lyrics onto chart paper and replace the words "orange orangutan" with new ones, such as "purple puppy." Then sing your new version together!

Magic Fairy

Sight Word: *of, one*

Vocabulary Words: *fairy, wand, poof*

Comprehension Boosters:

1. What is the child's first wish? What is the child's second wish?

2. Would you like to have 100 teddy bears? Why or why not?

Innovating the Text: Copy the lyrics onto chart paper and replace the word "teddies" with a new one, such as "kittens." Then sing your new version together!

I Can Get a Pet!

Sight Word: *or, how*

Vocabulary Words: *gerbil, walrus*

Comprehension Boosters:

1. Can you remember all the animals mentioned in the song? Make a list.

2. Do you think a walrus would make a good pet? Why or why not?

Innovating the Text: Copy the lyrics onto chart paper and replace the word "walrus" with a new one, such as "elephant." Then sing your new version together!

Fancy Mermaids

Sight Word: *from, had*

Vocabulary Words: *mermaids, dumplings, seaweed, crumpets*

Comprehension Boosters:
1. Who invited the mermaids to tea? (Hint: Look at the picture.)
2. What foods are served at this tea party? Do they sound yummy?

Innovating the Text:
Copy the lyrics onto chart paper and replace the words "fancy mermaids" with new ones, such as "cranky crabs." Then sing your new version together!

Harry Hamster

Sight Word: *at, but*

Vocabulary Words: *hamster, roam*

Comprehension Boosters:
1. What is the hamster's name?
2. Where did the child find her pet hamster? How does that make her feel?

Innovating the Text:
Copy the lyrics onto chart paper and replace the word "hamster" with a new animal, such as "lizard." Then sing your new version together!

Two Blue Cats

Sight Word: *they, have*

Vocabulary Words: *imagine, pride*

Comprehension Boosters:
1. What is special about these cats?
2. The cats live in Catmandu. Why is that a perfect place for them to live?

Innovating the Text:
Copy the lyrics onto chart paper and replace the words "two" and "blue" with a new

number and color, such as "three" and "green." Then sing your new version together!

Little Chick

Sight Word: *that, to*

Vocabulary Words: *peep, jeep, county fair*

Comprehension Boosters:
1. Is the story in this song real or pretend? How do you know?
2. This song includes two words that rhyme with *peep*. Can you find them? What other words rhyme with *peep*? Make a list.

Innovating the Text:
Copy the lyrics onto chart paper and replace the words "county fair" with a new destination, such as "shopping mall." Then sing your new version together!

Sue's Silly Shop

Sight Word: *for, which*

Vocabulary Words: *flavor, scoop, dandy*

Comprehension Boosters:
1. What does Sue's Silly Shop sell? What is silly about the shop?
2. What flavor of ice cream is your very favorite? Tell about it.

Innovating the Text:
Copy the lyrics onto chart paper and replace one or all of the ice cream flavors with new ones, such as "pickle" or "pizza." Then sing your new version together!

Did You Go to the Ocean?

Sight Words: *did, go*

Vocabulary Words: *snorkel, coral*

Comprehension Boosters:
1. Why do you think the narrator says, "Next time, PLEASE take me!"?
2. What sea creatures do you see in the picture? Make a list. Can you think of others?

Innovating the Text:
Copy the lyrics onto chart paper and replace "lemon fish" with a different sea creature, such as "sea turtle." Then sing your new version together!

Sight Word Song Book © Liza Charlesworth, Scholastic Inc.

My Painted Horse

Sight Words: *up, down*

Vocabulary Words: *carousel, gallop*

Comprehension Boosters:

1. What part of this song seems real? What part of this song seems imaginary (not real)?

2. Have you ever taken a ride on a carousel? Talk about it.

Innovating the Text:

Copy the lyrics onto chart paper and replace the direction words "up" and "down" with new words, such as "left" and "right." Then sing your new version together!

Deep in the Forest

Sight Word: *look, now*

Vocabulary Word: *flee*

Comprehension Boosters:

1. Is Big Foot friendly? How do you know?

2. Can you think of three or more words to describe Big Foot?

Innovating the Text:

Copy the lyrics onto chart paper and replace "Big Foot" with another real or imagined creature, such as "Scooby Doo." Then sing your new version together!

I'm a Little Pencil

Sight Word: *write, part*

Vocabulary Word: *tip*

Comprehension Boosters:

1. What does the little pencil write on the paper? Would you like to read it?

2. The pencil writes a story about elves, apes, ghosts, and magic grapes. Work together to write your own story that includes these four special items.

Innovating the Text:

Copy the lyrics onto chart paper and replace the story items "elves," "apes," "ghosts," and "magic grapes" with new ones. Then sing your new version together!

The Two Zoo

Sight Words: *see, two*

Vocabulary Words: *yaks, peacocks*

Comprehension Boosters:

1. Why is this zoo called the "Two Zoo"?

2. Do you think you'd see three lions or four bears at this zoo? Why or why not?

Innovating the Text:

Copy the lyrics onto chart paper and replace the word "two" with any number you choose. Then sing your new version together!

Monster Soup

Sight Words: *make, some*

Vocabulary Word: *slurp*

Comprehension Boosters:

1. Would you like to eat this monster soup? Why or why not?

2. What would you put in the monster soup?

Innovating the Text:

Copy the lyrics onto chart paper and replace the foods in this soup with new ones, such as "popcorn" or "hot dogs." Then sing your new version together!

Owl and Cow

Sight Words: *who, am*

Vocabulary Word: *questions*

Comprehension Boosters:

1. What question does the owl ask the cow? Why does it make sense for an owl to say "who"?

2. If you could ask a cow a question, what would it be?

Innovating the Text:

Copy the lyrics onto chart paper and replace "cow" and "MOO!" with a new animal/sound combo, such as "bear" and "GROWL!" Then sing your new version together!

Happy Hippo

Sight Words: *come, number*

Vocabulary Word: *"number one"*

Comprehension Boosters:

1. Can you remember all the things the child wants to do when Happy Hippo arrives? Make a list.

2. Would you like to play with Happy Hippo? Why or why not?

Innovating the Text:

Copy the lyrics onto chart paper and replace some or all of the play-date activities with new ones, such as "Come see my orange tree" or "Come pet my hamster." Then sing your new version together!

The Froggy Prince

Sight Words: *into, day*

Vocabulary Words: *pond, wand*

Comprehension Boosters:

1. What causes the frog to turn into a prince?

2. If you had a magic wand, what would you make happen?

Innovating the Text:

Copy the lyrics onto chart paper and replace the word "prince" with something else that the frog turns into, such as a "princess" or a "giraffe." Be sure to change the pronoun "he," if needed, as well. Then sing your new version together!

My Aunt Gert

Sight Words: *has, her*

Vocabulary Word: *glee*

Comprehension Boosters:

1. Do these animals really "talk"? How do they communicate?

2. Do the neighbors like Aunt Gert and her pets? How do you know?

Innovating the Text:

Copy the lyrics onto chart paper and replace one or more of the sounds and animals with new combos, such as "SSSSSS!" and "snake" or "GLUB!" and "fish." Then sing your new version together!

Dad Mouse

Sight Words: *been, time*

Vocabulary Words: *bale, dozing, mouselets*

Comprehension Boosters:

1. Why doesn't the mouse dad hear his mouse wife speaking?

2. Why do the mouselets want their dad to wake up? What do they want to do?

Innovating the Text:

Copy the lyrics onto chart paper and replace "mouse" and "mouselets" with a different animal/offspring combo, such as "bear" and "bear cubs." Then sing your new version together!

Double Bubbles

Sight Words: *get, then*

Vocabulary Word: *gobbled*

Comprehension Boosters:

1. What happens when one goat chews bubble gum?

What happens when two goats chew bubble gum?

2. Are there other ways to make bubbles? Talk about it.

Innovating the Text:

Copy the lyrics onto chart paper and replace "goat" and "goats" with a different type of animal, such as "dog/dogs" or "gorilla/gorillas." Then sing your new version together!

Croc Would Like

Sight Words: *would, could*

Vocabulary Word: *chomp*

Comprehension Boosters:

1. What does this crocodile do with the computer? Why is this surprising?

2. What other things might this silly crocodile like? What would he do with them?

Innovating the Text:

Copy the lyrics onto chart paper and replace the items that Croc wants, and what he does with them, with new combos, such as "ball" and "throw" or "car" and "drive." Then sing your new version together!

My Elf Pal

Sight Words: *my, out*

Vocabulary Words: *pour, pout, dashed*

Comprehension Boosters:

1. Why did the elf pal pout?

2. How did the elf pal feel when the sun came out? How do you know?

Innovating the Text:

Copy the lyrics onto chart paper and replace "eensy weensy" with a different way to describe a small elf, such as "teeny tiny" or "itty bitty." Then sing your new version together!

Penelope the Pig

Sight Words: *like, so*

Vocabulary Word: *fab*

Comprehension Boosters:

1. Can you think of three or more words to describe Penelope? Give it a try.

2. Would you like to have a pet crab like Penelope? Why or why not?

Innovating the Text:

Copy the lyrics onto chart paper and replace the clothing word "wig" and pet word "crab" with new words, such as "hat" and "frog." Then sing your new version together!

The Giant Family

Sight Words: *other, than*

Vocabulary Word: *giant*

Comprehension Boosters:

1. Who is the tallest giant in the family?

2. Would you like to be a giant? Talk about it.

Innovating the Text:
Copy the lyrics onto chart paper and replace the word "brother's" with "friend's." Change each giant's name to that of a student. Then sing your new version together!

Wiggle, Waggle, Woggle

Sight Words: *its, about*

Vocabulary Words: *woggle, hound*

Comprehension Boosters:

1. Can anyone spot the made-up word in this song? (*woggle*) Why do you think the author made up this word?

2. Do children have a special dog or other pet in their lives? Talk about it.

Innovating the Text:
Copy the lyrics onto chart paper and replace the word "woggle" with your own nonsense word to describe what the dog does. If you like, you can replace the word "snout," too. Then sing your new version together!

Who Goes First?

Sight Words: *first, these*

Vocabulary Word: *fair*

Comprehension Boosters:

1. Lou and Sue both want to go first. How do they fix their problem?

2. Lou and Sue are kind classmates. What are some other ways to be kind in the classroom?

Innovating the Text:
Copy the lyrics onto chart paper and replace the names "Lou," "Sue," and "Andrew" with the names of kids in your class. Then sing your new version together!

Zoom to Mars

Sight Words: *way, made*

Vocabulary Words: *Mars, Martian*

Comprehension Boosters:

1. Why is this child zooming to Mars? How do you think Mike Martian will feel about the visit?

2. Would you like to zoom to Mars? Talk about it.

Innovating the Text:
Copy the lyrics onto chart paper and replace the word "cake" with a different birthday surprise, such as "card" or "gift." Then sing your new version together!

Farm Pets

Sight Words: *may, call*

Vocabulary Word: *quite*

Comprehension Boosters:

1. What is surprising about the horse named Henry?

2. Would you like to have a talking horse for a pet? Talk about it.

Innovating the Text:
Copy the lyrics onto chart paper and replace one of the animals, plus its sound and name, with a new combo, such as "pig," "Petey," and "OINK!" Then sing your new version together!

Green Ghosties

Sight Words: *find, them*

Vocabulary Words:
ghosties, flip, rest

Comprehension Boosters:

1. What do the green ghosties do? How many of them are there?

2. Would you like to watch a green ghostie show? Talk about it.

Innovating the Text:
Copy the lyrics onto chart paper and replace the words "green" and "ghosties" with new color/ creature combos, such as "blue" and "batties." Then sing your new version together!

I Love You, Water

Sight Words: *water, no*

Vocabulary Words:
river, lake, bay

Comprehension Boosters:

1. How does water help flowers, fish, dolphins, and people? Find the answers in the song.

2. Why do you love water? Talk about it.

Innovating the Text:
Copy the lyrics onto chart paper and write a brand new stanza that celebrates water, such as "I love you, water, I love you, water!/I like to drink you on a hot day./I would be thirsty, so very thirsty./If water went away." Then sing your new version together!

Oscar the Octopus

Sight Words: *will, him*

Vocabulary Words: *octopus, star*

Comprehension Boosters:

1. Why does the song end by repeating the word "hand" eight times?

2. This song is about a pretend octopus. What facts do you know about real octopuses? Make a list.

Innovating the Text:
Copy the lyrics onto chart paper and replace "Oscar" with a new name that begins with a different letter of the alphabet, such as "Allie," "Bobby," or "Carlos." Discuss the letter and other words that begin with it. Then sing your new version together!

Sam Snowman

Sight Words: *more, long*

Vocabulary Word: *"half away"*

Comprehension Boosters:

1. Why did the snowman melt half away?

2. Do you like to eat ice cream? Talk about it.

Innovating the Text:
Copy the lyrics onto chart paper and replace the word "ice cream" with a different treat, such as "popcorn" or "pickles." Then sing your new version together!

The Rain Forest Tree

Sight Words: *many, people*

Vocabulary Word: *rain forest*

Comprehension Boosters:

1. The boy in this song wishes that people could be in the rain forest tree. How is this problem solved?

2. Would you like to spend time in this special tree, too? Talk about it.

Innovating the Text:
Copy the lyrics onto chart paper and replace one or more of the rain forest animal types with new ones, such as "butterflies" or "lizards." Then sing your new version together!

Monster Food

(Sung to "This Old Man")

He is Nate.

He can't wait

to gobble up what's on his plate:

Dirty socks and rocks

and worms and sticky tape.

He thinks monster food is great!

15

The Sneaky Snake

(Sung to "There Were Three Jolly Fisherman")

There was a very sneaky snake.

There was a very sneaky snake.

Very sneaky, snake, snake, snake

watched the baker bake, bake, bake.

There was a very sneaky snake!

There was a very yummy cake.

There was a very yummy cake.

But the very sneaky, snake, snake, snake

ate the baker's cake, cake, cake.

And now he has a bellyache!

Sight Word Song Book © Liza Charlesworth, Scholastic Inc.

The Cookie Boy

(Sung to "My Bonnie Lies Over the Ocean")

The cookie said, "I am so clever."

The cookie said, "I am so quick."

The cookie said, "You'll never catch me."

Then off cookie ran, lickety-split!

Away, away.

The cookie went running away to play!

Away, away.

Then fox said, "I'll eat you today."

CRUNCH!

Gilly Ghosty

is when

(Sung to "She'll Be Coming 'Round the Mountain")

Gilly Ghosty is a baby, that is true.

Gilly Ghosty is a baby, that is true.

And when he gets a little hungry,

when he gets a little hungry,

then he begins to holler, "BOO-HOO-HOO!"

Gilly Ghosty is a baby, that is true.

Gilly Ghosty is a baby, that is true.

And when he gets a little bottle,

when he gets a little bottle,

then he begins to babble, "BOO-GOO-GOO!"

Sight Word Song Book © Liza Charlesworth, Scholastic Inc.

Pirate Song

(Sung to "Ta Ra Ra Boom De Ay")

This is a pirate song,

and you can sing along.

So use a pirate voice,

that is the salty choice.

Use words like MATE and AYE.

Say SCALLYWAG today.

Use words like BLIMEY, too,

'cause that's what pirates do!

Use words like YO HO HO.

Use words like THAR SHE BLOWS.

And at the very end,

say ARGHH and start again!

19

Furry Little Mice

(Sung to "Twinkle, Twinkle Little Star")

We are furry little mice,

and we are very, very nice.

We are cute and we can squeak.

So why do people shout out, "EEK"?

We are furry little mice,

and we are very, very nice.

Ben's Band

(Sung to "Oh, Susanna")

Ben came from the country

with a banjo on his knee,

and his pig, whose name was Pickle,

and his lamb, whose name was Lee,

and his cow, whose name was Clover,

and his mouse, whose name was Min,

and when they sang together,

it would always make me grin.

"OINK, BAA, MOO, SQUEAK!"

That was their happy tune.

They sang their song together

underneath the crescent moon.

Where Is Humpty?

(Sung to "Are You Sleeping?")

what
as

Where is Humpty, where is Humpty?

On the wall, on the wall.

Oops, he tumbled over.

Oops, he tumbled over.

What a fall, what a fall!

How is Humpty, how is Humpty?

As good as new, as good as new.

He is back together.

He is back together.

What great glue, what great glue!

The Talking Gnu

(Sung to "Do You Know the Muffin Man?")

Do you know the talking gnu,

the talking gnu, whose name is Lou?

Do you know the talking gnu

who lives at Chatty Zoo?

Do you know the talking gnu,

the talking gnu, whose name is Lou?

Do you know the talking gnu?

Lou says that he knows you!

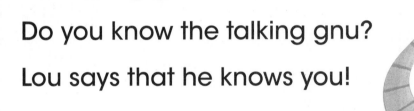

On Top of My Sandwich

(Sung to "On Top of Old Smokey")

On top of my sandwich, all covered with ham,

I put on some meatballs and strawberry jam.

I put on some pickles and nice stinky cheese.

I put on some noodles and little green peas.

I put on some cookies and gumdrops of blue.

I put on some mustard and some ketchup, too.

I asked my big brother to please take a bite.

But he said, "No thank you, that wouldn't be right."

Mary Had a Hairy Ape

a
she

(Sung to "Mary Had a Little Lamb")

Mary had a hairy ape,

a hairy ape, a hairy ape.

Mary had a hairy ape.

She thought that ape was great!

And when she gave him a guitar,

a guitar, a guitar,

when she gave him a guitar,

that ape became a star!

Read Your Book

(Sung to "Row, Row, Row Your Boat")

Read, read, read your book

with your mom or dad.

It's about this big bad wolf—

he'll really make you mad!

Read, read, read your book

with your pals at school.

It's about this magic frog

inside a golden pool!

Read, read, read your book

with your favorite aunt.

It's about this little boy

who climbs a giant plant!

Read, read, read your book

with your best-est friend

It's about this glass slipper—

don't tell me how it ends!

Sight Word Song Book © Liza Charlesworth, Scholastic Inc.

Pete Penguin

(Sung to "Here We Go 'Round the Mulberry Bush")

Pete Penguin waddled by the sea

by the sea, by the sea.

Pete Penguin waddled by the sea

and he said this to me:

"Will you come and play with me,

play with me, play with me?

We can skate and sled and ski

and waddle by the sea."

Yippee!

Ruby Robin

(Sung to "Clementine")

Ruby Robin, Ruby Robin

is as lovely as can be.

She can fly and she can flutter,

she can sing so prettily.

Ruby Robin, Ruby Robin

is as lovely as can be.

She sings, "Can you come for supper?"

But a worm is not for me!

Goldilocks, Goldilocks

(Sung to "Billy Boy")

Do not go in that house,

Goldilocks, Goldilocks!

Do not go in that house,

you'll get in trouble!

You'll eat porridge, break a chair,

snooze in bed and wake to bears…

then get so scared,

you'll run away forever.

Little Dot

(Sung to "Miss Susie Had a Baby")

This song's about a dino,

whose name is Little Dot.

Dot was pink all over

with lots of purple spots.

Dot loved math and reading.

She thought all kids were cool.

So she bought a backpack

and stomped all the way to school.

When Dot got to the classroom,

kids didn't know what to think—

'cause they were taught in science

all the dinos were extinct!

all
were

Frog and Dog

(Sung to "If You're Happy and You Know It")

if
it

If you're hoppy and you know it,

you're a frog.

If you're hoppy and you know it,

you're a frog.

If you jump and swim and play

and say RIBBIT every day—

If you're hoppy and you know it,

you're a frog.

If you're yappy and you know it,

you're a dog.

If you're yappy and you know it,

you're a dog.

If you eat and sleep and play

and say BOW WOW every day—

If you're yappy and you know it,

you're a dog.

Orange Orangutan

(Sung to "Oh, Dear! What Can the Matter Be?")

I'm an orange orangutan.

I drive around in a jungle van.

Each day, I go play with Tarzan.

We swing on the jungle vines!

Each day we play, we have

oh, such an awesome time.

Each day we play, we have

oh, such an awesome time.

Each day we play, we have

oh, such an awesome time.

We swing on the jungle vines!

Wheeeeeeeeeeeee!

Magic Fairy

(Sung to "Reuben, Reuben")

Magic Fairy, I've been thinking

of one wish I'd like today.

I REALLY want one hundred teddies.

Wave your wand and make my day!

POOF!

Magic Fairy, I've been thinking

of one wish I got today.

One hundred teddies are TOO many.

Please take ninety-nine away!

POOF!

I Can Get a Pet!

(Sung to "The Farmer in the Dell")

or how

A dog or a cat?

A dog or a cat?

Dad said I can get a pet.

Imagine that!

A gerbil or a chick?

A gerbil or a chick?

Dad said I can get a pet.

But how do I pick?

A frog or a mouse?

A frog or a mouse?

Dad said I can get a pet

to keep inside the house.

A bird or a fish?

A bird or a fish?

How do I tell Daddy

that a walrus is my wish?

Fancy Mermaids

(Sung to "Are You Sleeping?")

from
had

Fancy mermaids, fancy mermaids,

from the sea, from the sea.

I had to invite you,

I had to invite you

to come for tea, tea with me.

Fancy mermaids, fancy mermaids,

from the sea, from the sea.

We had ocean dumplings

and salty seaweed crumpets.

Yum-yummy! Yum-yummy!

Harry Hamster

(Sung to "Baa, Baa, Black Sheep")

Harry Hamster, where are you?

At a park or at a zoo?

At a mall or Timbuktu

or sailing on the ocean blue?

I know you really like to roam,

but I miss you at my home.

Harry Hamster, I found you

snoozing in my favorite shoe!

You had me worried, that is true,

but you look cute, you really do.

When I lost you, I was sad

but now I'm very, very glad!

Two Blue Cats

(Sung to "Three Blind Mice")

they have

Two blue cats, two blue cats,

imagine that, imagine that!

They have blue eyes and ears, they do.

They have blue paws and whiskers, too.

They are the pride of Catmandu—

Those two blue cats!

WELCOME TO CATMANDU

Little Chick

(Sung to "Old MacDonald")

that
to

Once there was a little chick

that went PEEP, PEEP, PEEP.

He liked to drive a little jeep

that went BEEP, BEEP, BEEP.

With a PEEP, PEEP here

and a BEEP, BEEP there,

he drove that jeep

to the county fair.

Once there was a little chick

that went PEEP, PEEP, PEEP.

38

Sue's Silly Shop

(Sung to "Yankee Doodle")

I went to Sue's Silly Shop

for a scoop of ice cream.

But which flavor should I pick?

There were one hundred nineteen!

Oh, which flavor should I pick—

popcorn or cotton candy?

Oh, which flavor should I pick?

My, they all looked dandy!

I went to Sue's Silly Shop

for a scoop of ice cream.

But which flavor should I pick?

Each sounded like a sweet dream!

Oh, which flavor should I pick,

cupcake or minty candy?

Oh, I have decided now—

a scoop of each is dandy!

Sight Word Song Book © Liza Charlesworth, Scholastic Inc.

Did You Go to the Ocean?

(Sung to "Do Your Ears Hang Low")

Did you go to the ocean?

Did you go to the sea?

Did you go to swim with dolphins?

Did you go to water ski?

Did you snorkel through the coral

with a lemon fish named Lee?

Next time, PLEASE take me!

My Painted Horse

(Sung to "The Wheels on the Bus")

My painted horse goes up and down,

up and down, up and down.

My painted horse goes up and down

and round and round and round.

My painted horse goes up and down,

up and down, up and down.

Then we leave the carousel

and gallop through the town!

up down

Deep in the Forest

(Sung to "Rock-a-Bye Baby")

Deep in the forest, what do I see?

Look! It is Big Foot behind a tree.

Look! He is hairy, as hairy can be.

Now he is walking, walking toward me.

How my heart pounds, how I want to flee,

'cause now he is talking, talking to me!

"I know I look scary," he says sweetly.

"But I just came over to bring you some tea."

I'm a Little Pencil

(Sung to "I'm a Little Teapot")

I'm a little pencil,

tall and thin.

Tip me over—

I'll begin.

On a sheet of paper,

flat and white,

watch me write and

write and write!

There's a part about elves,

and a part about apes,

and a part about ghosts,

and three magic grapes.

And now my story

is all done.

You can read it.

Oh, what fun!

write part

I'm a little pencil

tall

The Two Zoo

(Sung to "Take Me Out to the Ball Game")

see two

Take me out to the Two Zoo!

It is a great place to be.

I see two bats and two kangaroos.

I see two tigers and two yaks, too.

I see two bears and two zebras

and two pretty peacocks of blue.

How I love to go to the zoo

and see all those twos!

Monster Soup

(Sung to "Make New Friends")

Monster will make soup for you—

in go cherries and some cheese, too.

Monster will make soup for you—

in go pickles and some peas, too.

Monster will make soup for you—

in go meatballs and some milk, too.

Monster will make soup for you—

in go cookies and some cakes, too.

Monster has made soup for you.

Slurp it up and say, "Thank you!"

SLURP! Thank you!

Owl and Cow

(Sung to "Bingo")

The spotted owl up in the tree

asked the cow some questions.

"Who, who, who are you?"

"Who, who, who are you?"

"Who, who, who are you?"

"And what is it you do?"

The spotted cow down on the ground

answered all the questions.

"I am a cow, that's who."

"I am a cow, that's who."

"I am a cow, that's who."

"And this is what I do—

MOOOOOOOOOOOOOOOOOOOOO!"

Happy Hippo

(Sung to "Playmate, Come Out and Play With Me")

come number

Hey, Happy Hippo!

Come by and play with me.

Come see my cherry tree.

Come sip my apple tea.

Come crunch some cookies.

Just knock on my front door,

you'll be my number one forever more!

Hey, Happy Hippo!

Come by and play with me.

Come see my turtles, three.

Come meet my sister, Dee.

Come play some board games.

Just stomp across my floor,

you'll be my number one forever more!

The Froggy Prince

(Sung to "The Ants Go Marching")

The froggy jumped into a pond,

one day in May!

The froggy jumped into a pond,

one day in May!

The froggy jumped into a pond,

a fairy waved her magic wand—

then he turned into a prince with a crown

and a castle in town.

Hey, hey, hey!

Sight Word Song Book © Liza Charlesworth, Scholastic Inc.

My Aunt Gert

(Sung to "Six Little Ducks")

has
her

My Aunt Gert has a cat and a dog,

and she has a bird,

and she has a frog.

When she takes them for a walk—

all they do is talk, talk, talk.

"MEOW!" says her cat.

"ARF!" says her dog.

"TWEET!" says her bird.

"RIBBIT!" says her frog.

Then her neighbors shout with glee,

"What a chatty family!"

TWEET!

RIBBIT!

ARF!

MEOW!

Dad Mouse

(Sung to "I've Been Working on the Railroad")

Dad mouse has been sleeping
on a bale of hay.
Dad mouse has been sleeping
just to pass the time away.

Can't he hear his mouse wife speaking,
"You've been dozing all day!"
Can't he hear his mouselets squeaking,
"It's time for us to play!"

Double Bubbles

get then

(Sung to "Pop Goes the Weasel")

One goat gobbled up some gum

and didn't get in trouble.

Then he chewed and then he blew—

POP

went a bubble!

Two goats gobbled up some gum

and didn't get in trouble.

Then they chewed and then they blew—

POP-POP

went double bubbles!

Croc Would Like

(Sung to "London Bridge")

Croc would like a cowboy hat,
cowboy hat, cowboy hat.
Croc would like a cowboy hat,
so he could wear it.

Croc would like a comic book,
comic book, comic book.
Croc would like a comic book,
so he could read it.

Croc would like a computer,
computer, computer.
Croc would like a computer,
so he could eat it.

CHOMP!

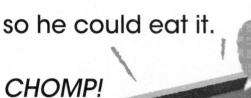

My Elf Pal

(Sung to "The Eensy Weensy Spider")

my
out

My eensy weensy elf pal

wanted to go out.

But it began to pour,

which made my elf pal pout.

Then out came the sun,

and there was rain no more.

So he hopped into my pocket,

and we dashed out my door!

Penelope the Pig

(Sung to "John Jacob Jingleheimer Schmidt")

like
so

I am Penelope the Pig.

I like to wear my wig.

Whenever I go out,

people like to shout,

"That wig is so,

so, so, so BIG!"

I am Penelope the Pig.

I like to walk my crab.

Whenever I go out,

people like to shout,

"That crab is so,

so, so, so FAB!"

Sight Word Song Book © Liza Charlesworth, Scholastic Inc.

The Giant Family

(Sung to "Skip to My Lou")

other than

My brother's name is Bill.

My other brother's name is Will.

My other brother's name is Gill.

We're giants on a hill!

Will is taller than brother Bill.

Gill is taller than brother Will.

And I'm taller than brother Gill

'cause I'm giant Jill!

Sight Word Song Book © Liza Charlesworth, Scholastic Inc.

Wiggle, Waggle, Woggle

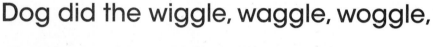

its about

(Sung to "Hokey Pokey")

The dog wiggled its ears.

The dog waggled its tail.

The dog woggled its snout

and went barking all about.

Dog did the wiggle, waggle, woggle,

and it makes us want to shout,

"A hound's what this song's about!"

Who Goes First?

(Sung to "Happy Birthday to You")

first
these

"I go first!" said Lou.

"I go first!" said Lou.

"I go first!" said Lou.

"That's not fair!" said Sue.

"I go first!" said Sue.

"I go first!" said Sue.

"I go first!" said Sue.

"That's not fair!" said Lou.

What did these pals do?

What did these pals do?

They fixed it by saying,

"You go first, Andrew!"

Zoom to Mars

(Sung to "Buffalo Girls Can You Come Out Tonight?")

Mars is such a long, long way,

long, long way, long, long way.

Mars is such a long, long way,

but I'll zoom there today.

I'll take along a cake I made,

cake I made, cake I made.

I'll take along a cake I made

for Mike Martian's birthday!

Happy Birthday, Mike!

MEEP, MEEP!

Farm Pets

(Sung to "Sing a Song of Sixpence")

I may get a pet lamb,
yes, I really may.
I will call him Larry.
"BAAA!" is what he'll say.

I may get a pet chick,
yes, I really may.
I will call him Charley.
"PEEP!" is what he'll say.

I may get a pet horse,
yes, I really may.
I will call him Henry,
"HELLO!" is what he'll say.

Then, Henry may ask me,
"How are you today?"
For Henry is a talking horse
with quite a lot to say!

Green Ghosties

(Sung to "Down by the Station")

find them

I go to the old tree
to find green ghosties.
Do I find them?
No, no, no!

I go to the old house
to find green ghosties.
Do I find them?
Yes, yes, yes!

I watch them flip
and fly and rest.
Green ghosties are
the best, best, best!
Boooooo!

I Love You, Water

(Sung to "You Are My Sunshine")

I love you, water. I love you, water!

You fall on gardens, when skies are gray.

There'd be no roses, there'd be no daisies—

if water went away!

I love you, water. I love you, water!

You fill the river and lake and bay.

There'd be no goldfish, there'd be no dolphins—

if water went away!

I love you, water. I love you, water!

You become snowflakes on a cold day.

There'd be no snowmen, there'd be no snowballs—

if water went away!

Oscar the Octopus

(Sung to "Heads, Shoulders, Knees, and Toes")

will
him

Oscar the Octopus, you will love him!

Oscar the Octopus, you will love him!

He's a big star. You will be his fan.

And you can even shake his hand—

hand hand hand hand hand hand hand!

Sam Snowman

more
long

(Sung to "The Bear Went Over the Mountain")

Sam Snowman wanted more ice cream.

Sam Snowman wanted more ice cream.

Sam Snowman wanted more ice cream,

so he slid to the store.

It was a hot, hot day.

It was a long, long way.

So by the time he'd gotten more ice cream,

by the time he'd gotten more ice cream,

by the time he'd gotten more ice cream—

Sam melted half away!

The Rain Forest Tree

(Sung to "Hush, Little Baby")

I see so many birds in the rain forest tree!

I wish it was a place for people to be.

I see so many chimps in the rain forest tree!

I wish it was a place for people to be.

I see so many frogs in the rain forest tree!

I wish it was a place for people to be.

So I'm building a house in the rain forest tree.

Now it'll be a place for animals and ME!